PRESENT
not perfect
FOR PREGNANCY

A MINDFULNESS JOURNAL
FOR MOTHERS—TO—BE

Aimee Chase,
author of *Present Not Perfect*

CASTLE POINT BOOKS
NEW YORK

PRESENT, NOT PERFECT FOR PREGNANCY. Copyright © 2019 by
St. Martin's Press. All rights reserved. Printed in the United States of America.
For information, address St. Martin's Press, 120 Broadway, New York, NY 10271.

www.castlepointbooks.com

The Castle Point Books trademark is owned by Castle Point Publishing, LLC.
Castle Point books are published and distributed by St. Martin's Press.

ISBN 978-1-250-22866-6 (trade paperback)

Our books may be purchased in bulk for promotional, educational, or business
use. Please contact your local bookseller or the Macmillan Corporate and
Premium Sales Department at 1-800-221-7945, extension 5442, or by email
at MacmillanSpecialMarkets@macmillan.com.

First Edition: October 2019

10 9 8 7 6 5 4 3 2 1

THIS JOURNAL BELONGS TO

INTRODUCTION

PRACTICE MINDFULNESS and enjoy some Zen moments with *Present, not Perfect for Pregnancy*. This daily reflection journal will help you stay centered and self-aware from the first trimester to the last. Each page offers a personal prompt or a lighthearted quote to awaken gratitude, inner strength, positivity, and confidence whenever you need it.

Find the pages that move you and fill them with your true thoughts and feelings. Allow the judgments of others (and your own inner critic) to fall away as you resolve to embrace your perfectly imperfect life and the unpredictable, heart-soaring adventure of pregnancy. And finally, prepare for the arrival of the most amazing miracle that life can bring.

HEART IN MY HAND

....

CLOSE YOUR EYES AND LET YOUR MIND GO QUIET.
FOCUS ON YOUR BREATHING UNTIL YOU FEEL CENTERED
AND CALM. PRESS A HAND TO YOUR BELLY AND IMAGINE
THAT YOU CAN HEAR YOUR BABY'S HEARTBEAT.

WRITE DOWN ANY THOUGHTS AND FEELINGS
THAT AROSE WHILE YOU MEDITATED.

IF ANY NEGATIVE THOUGHTS OR WORRIES POPPED INTO
YOUR HEAD, DON'T JUDGE YOURSELF FOR THEM. WHAT MIGHT
THEY EXPRESS ABOUT YOUR FEARS AS AN EXPECTING MOM?

HOW DO YOU LOVE YOUR BABY?
COUNT THE WAYS BELOW:

1.

2.

3.

4.

5.

6.

7.

8.

SEIZE THIS MOMENT TO BOND WITH YOUR BABY.
WRITE A SHORT LETTER BELOW. EXPLAIN HOW MUCH
YOUR BABY MEANS TO YOU AND DESCRIBE WHAT MAKES
YOU MOST EXCITED ABOUT BEING HIS/HER MOM.

DEAR   ,

LOVE, YOUR MOM

Finding Fulfillment

People often talk about pregnancy food cravings,
but we can also crave a feeling or an experience.
What emotional cravings are you having right now?
Circle any and all that apply. Make a list below:

LOVE　　　　　　**COMPANIONSHIP**

ALONE TIME　　　　　　**SLEEP**

REASSURANCE　　　　　　**ROMANCE**

What experiences or activities
do you enjoy now more than ever?

THROUGH THE EYES OF GRATITUDE,

everything is a miracle.

—MARY DAVIS

WRITE A SHORT MESSAGE TO YOUR PAST SELF.
TELL HER HOW FAR YOU HAVE COME. TELL HER HOW LUCKY
SHE WILL FEEL TO BE YOU IN THIS MOMENT.

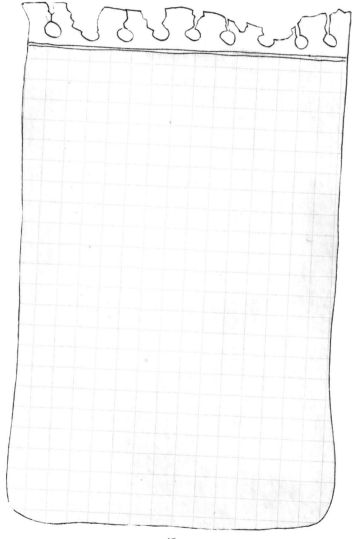

NOTHING AWAKENS US TO THE PRESENT MOMENT MORE THAN A NEW EXPERIENCE. Use the diagram below to compare your pre-pregnant mindset to your current mindset. Describe your pre-pregnancy goals, priorities, and attitude in the lower circle. Fill in the upper circle with your newly awakened goals, priorities, and attitude. What, if anything, has shifted?

What surprised you about pregnancy?

What didn't surprise you about pregnancy?

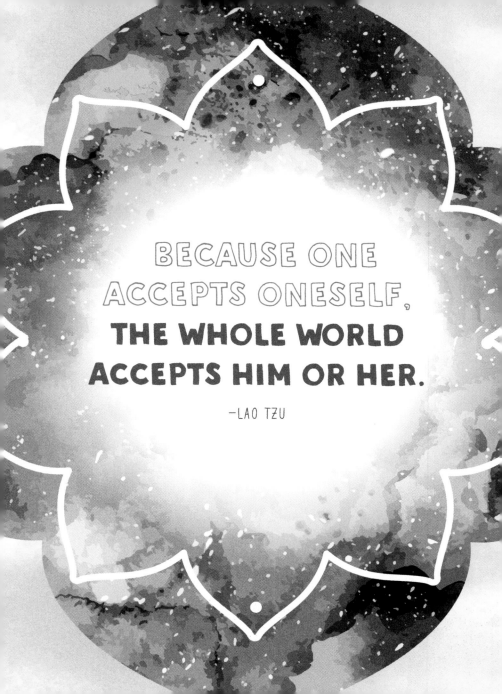

WRITE A MESSAGE TO YOUR PRESENT SELF.
MAKE IT AS ENCOURAGING AND ACCEPTING AS YOU CAN,
AND REPEAT THIS MESSAGE ANY TIME YOU NEED A BOOST.

**YOU ARE PERFECT
JUST THE WAY YOU ARE.**

YOU'VE GOT THIS.

YOU ARE FULL OF LOVE.

BEING MINDFUL MEANS BEING AWARE THAT TIME IS FLEETING,
AND THAT "RIGHT NOW" IS OF GREATEST IMPORTANCE AND VALUE.
Reserve time each day to slow down and
take stock of your inner and outer world. Pull back
your judgments and simply be. Starting now.

What's going on inside of you today?
What thoughts keep surfacing?

What small miracles or points of beauty can
you find in the world around you?

PREGNANCY IS A GIFT THAT HEIGHTENS THE SENSES.
WHICH OF YOUR SENSES HAVE BEEN SHARPENED BY THE
EXPERIENCE OF PREGNANCY?

SIGHT   SMELL

HEARING

TOUCH   TASTE

CHOOSE ONE OF YOUR SHARPEST SENSES AND USE IT TO GROUND
YOURSELF IN THE PRESENT MOMENT. WHAT ARE YOU AWARE OF
ABOUT THE WORLD AROUND YOU? WRITE A DESCRIPTION BELOW:

WHAT OTHER GIFTS HAS PREGNANCY GIVEN YOU?
WRITE THEM ON THE PRESENTS BELOW:

THE LIFE OF A MOTHER
IS THE LIFE OF A CHILD:
YOU ARE TWO BLOSSOMS
ON A SINGLE BRANCH.

—KAREN MAEZEN MILLER

WHEN ARE YOU MOST AWARE OF YOUR BABY'S COMPANY?

WHAT DOES IT FEEL LIKE TO BE EXPERIENCING LIFE
AS TWO PEOPLE RATHER THAN ONE?

EMBRACE THIS CHANGE in your life wholeheartedly. Let go of the past by writing down three things you left behind when you became pregnant. Look for joy in the present as you list three new sources of joy.

THINGS I MISS DOING

NEW THINGS I ENJOY

1.

2.

3.

1.

2.

3.

PREGNANCY [IS] A TIME OF *transition,* GROWTH, AND PROFOUND BEGINNINGS.

—ANNE CHRISTIAN BUCHANAN

Emotions are the great captains of our lives.

—VINCENT VAN GOGH

EMOTIONS CARRY US TO IMPORTANT PLACES. WHETHER YOU HAVE A BABBLING BROOK, A RISING RIVER, OR RAGING RAPIDS INSIDE YOU TODAY, LET THOSE FEELINGS TAKE YOU SOMEWHERE AS YOU DESCRIBE THEM ON THE WAVES BELOW.

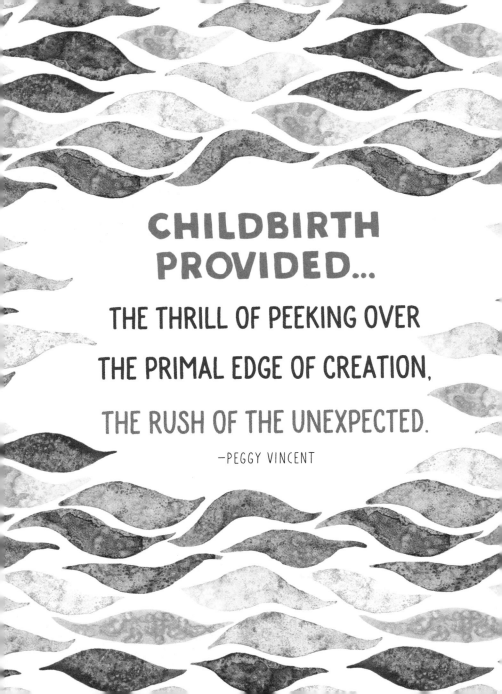

CHILDBIRTH PROVIDED...

THE THRILL OF PEEKING OVER THE PRIMAL EDGE OF CREATION, THE RUSH OF THE UNEXPECTED.

—PEGGY VINCENT

EMOTIONS GIVE US SELF-AWARENESS AND SELF-AWARENESS IS STRENGTH. SURRENDERING TO A FEELING IS A SMALL ACT OF COURAGE.

How do emotions make you stronger?

TRUST
YOURSELF

WHEN DO YOU TRUST YOURSELF MOST?

WHO HAS COMPLETE FAITH IN YOU?

THE NEXT TIME YOU'RE DOUBTING YOUR
ABILITIES OR INSTINCTS, IMAGINE WHAT ANY
OF THE PEOPLE ABOVE WOULD SAY TO YOU.

LIST ALL OF THE SOLICITED AND UNSOLICITED ADVICE
YOU'VE RECEIVED ABOUT PREGNANCY AND
PARENTHOOD ON THE ROAD SIGNS BELOW.

BE YOUR OWN BEST GUIDE AND MANEUVER YOUR WAY
TO NEW PARENTHOOD ON YOUR TERMS. WRITE YOUR
BEST ADVICE TO YOURSELF ON THE PATH BELOW.

USE A SIMPLE SOUND TO FEEL
CENTERED AND AT PEACE TODAY.

Play a sound that relaxes you. Maybe it's a reverberating
gong or ocean sounds. Allow yourself to do nothing but listen
and breathe in through your nose and out through your mouth
for three relaxing minutes. Let your thoughts take form,
but always return to the natural flow of your breath.
If it helps you to relax, repeat a phrase in your mind like:

I am not my thoughts; or *All I have to do is breathe.*

What did you notice as you experimented
with mindful meditation?

If you want
to conquer the
anxiety of life,
LIVE IN THE
MOMENT,
LIVE IN
THE BREATH.

—AMIT RAY

LOOK FOR A CONNECTION TO NATURE TODAY.

Notice the life outside your body as you consider the
life growing within. Drink tea on your front steps before
anyone else is awake, take a long, thoughtful walk through the
park, or step out into the night to take in the beauty of
the moon and stars. You're a sacred part of this vast universe.

What natural surroundings help to calm you?

What answers are you looking for right now?

What time of day would work best for a nature break?

BE SURE TO FIND YOUR HAPPY PLACE IN NATURE
AS MUCH AS POSSIBLE. IF IT CAN'T BE PART OF YOUR
EVERYDAY ROUTINE, THEN MAKE IT A WEEKLY GOAL.

YOUR BODY IS EXPERTLY DESIGNED to help your baby grow and anticipate your little one's changing needs. How has your body already adapted to help nurture your baby? What differences, both subtle and pronounced, have you noticed?

What do you love most about your pregnant body?

WHETHER IT'S A BUBBLE BATH, WORDS
OF GRATITUDE, OR A YOGA CLASS, FIND A WAY
TO CELEBRATE OR HONOR YOUR BODY TODAY.

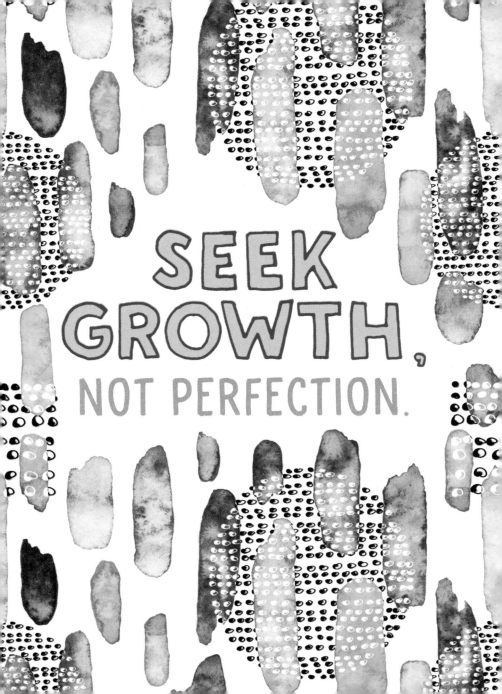

Giving grace to yourself

IS NEVER MORE IMPORTANT THAN
WHEN YOU BECOME A MOTHER.

—WHITNEY MEADE

RESIST THE TEMPTATION TO DO IT ALL DURING YOUR
PREGNANCY. REACH OUT AND ACCEPT SUPPORT WHEN YOU NEED IT.

STOP FOR A MOMENT TO CONSIDER HOW YOUR
PARTNER AND/OR OTHERS CAN HELP YOU STAY AFLOAT.
WHAT KIND OF HELP COULD YOU USE MOST?

WHO COULD YOU REACH OUT TO
FOR SUPPORT WHEN YOU NEED IT?

EXAMINE YOUR EXPECTATIONS TODAY AND
CONSIDER YOUR IDEALS RELATING TO FAMILY.

DESCRIBE THE KIND OF MOTHER YOU WANT TO BE.

DESCRIBE THE KIND OF PARENT YOU WANT YOUR PARTNER TO BE.

WHAT HAVE YOU LEARNED ABOUT YOUR RELATIONSHIPS
SINCE BECOMING PREGNANT?

WHAT, IF ANYTHING, ARE YOU HOLDING BACK
FROM SAYING TO YOUR PARTNER?

*Life is
a balance*
BETWEEN HOLDING ON
AND LETTING GO.

—RUMI

MOTHERHOOD IS A BALANCING ACT. REFLECT ON THE
CURRENT BALANCE OF YOUR LIFE AS YOU LIST YOUR VALUES AND
DESCRIBE HOW YOU SPEND YOUR FREE TIME BELOW. WHAT SMALL
CHANGES CAN YOU MAKE TO BETTER ALIGN THESE TWO LISTS?

THINGS I CARE
ABOUT MOST

HOW I SPEND
MOST OF MY TIME

LOVE
YOURSELF
WITH
ALL
YOU'VE
GOT

FIND AN ARTFUL WAY TO PAY TRIBUTE TO YOUR INCREDIBLE, LIFE-GIVING BODY TODAY.

Measure your growing belly on a length of ribbon, trace your shadow on the ground in chalk, or simply attach a beautiful photo of your pregnant body here.

Add positive words and praise for your body around the edges of your image.

GORGEOUS

WOMANLY

STRONG

NATURAL

BEAUTIFUL

MIRACULOUS

HAPPINESS
is all
around you

WRITE DOWN (IN BRIGHTLY COLORED PEN)
3 THINGS YOU ARE ENJOYING AT THIS STAGE OF PREGNANCY.

1.

2.

3.

WRITE DOWN (IN PENCIL)
3 WORRIES YOU HAVE ABOUT THE FUTURE.

1.

2.

3.

IMAGINE THAT YOUR FEARS AND WORRIES ABOUT THE FUTURE
ARE UNWARRANTED AND THAT EVERYTHING TURNS OUT OKAY.
ERASE THE ITEMS ON THE SECOND LIST ONE BY ONE AND LET GO
OF YOUR DESIRE TO CONTROL WHAT YOU CAN'T CONTROL.

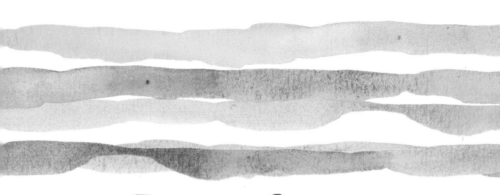

I sit here...
and wonder
WHO IN THE WORLD YOU
WILL TURN OUT TO BE.

—CARRIE FISHER

IMAGINE WHAT YOUR BABY IS SEEING OR EXPERIENCING AT THIS MOMENT.

Add an ultrasound image below if it helps you to imagine.
Describe the world inside of you from the point of view of your baby.

Marvel at the "wow" moments that have
punctuated your pregnancy. Describe one here.

PREGNANT · and · POWERFUL

LIST ALL THE WAYS IN WHICH PREGNANCY MAKES YOU FEEL EMPOWERED.

That first pregnancy

IS A LONG SEA JOURNEY

TO A COUNTRY

WHERE YOU DON'T

KNOW THE LANGUAGE.

—EMILY PERKINS

IF YOU COULD DESCRIBE YOUR
PREGNANCY JOURNEY IN JUST A FEW WORDS,
WHICH WORDS WOULD YOU CHOOSE?

HOW DO YOU THINK THE EXPERIENCE MIGHT
CHANGE YOU? WHAT LANGUAGE OR SECRETS
DO YOU HOPE TO DISCOVER?

WHAT GOOD MOTHERS AND
FATHERS INSTINCTIVELY FEEL
LIKE DOING FOR THEIR BABIES
**IS USUALLY BEST
AFTER ALL.**

—BENJAMIN SPOCK

BEING AN EXPECTANT MOM IS A BIG JOB, BUT YOU'VE GOT THIS.

Take this moment to remind yourself that you are the best captain of this ship for two, and that everything you need to know is imprinted somewhere within. Think of all the things you have done right so far in this pregnancy and write them between the spokes of the wheel.

TAKE A DEEP BREATH AND STAND PROUDLY AT THE HELM.

At the touch of love,
EVERYONE
BECOMES A
POET.

—PLATO

58

WRITE A POEM OR JOURNAL ENTRY
THAT EXPRESSES HOW YOU FEEL ABOUT
YOUR BABY OR YOUR PREGNANCY TODAY.

FIND YOUR BLISS

CHOOSE FROM THIS LIST OF BLISSFUL ACTIVITIES, AND ADD
SOME OF YOUR OWN PERSONAL WAYS FOR FINDING BLISS.

TAKING A SOOTHING BATH

READING QUIETLY

SLEEPING LATE

WATCHING THE SUNRISE/SUNSET

OBSERVING THE NIGHT SKY

HOW MIGHT YOU ADD SOME OF THE ABOVE TO YOUR WEEK?

CHOOSE AN IMAGE THAT CAN HELP YOU FIND PEACE. IT CAN
BE A VACATION SPOT, A SET OF WINDCHIMES, A BEST FRIEND,
A SLEEPING NEWBORN, OR ANYTHING ELSE THAT GIVES YOU A SENSE
OF CALM. DRAW OR DESCRIBE YOUR CALMING IMAGE BELOW.

VISUALIZE THIS ITEM (OR PLACE) TO SUMMON INNER CALM WHENEVER YOU NEED IT: ON THE SUBWAY, AT THE DOCTOR'S OFFICE, OR WAITING IN LINE AT THE POST OFFICE. ALLOW EVERYTHING THAT GIVES YOU STRESS TO FADE INTO THE BACKGROUND AS YOU ENJOY YOUR CALMING VISION.

EXPLAIN WHY YOU CHOSE THIS IMAGE.

PREGNANCY BRINGS ALL SORTS OF SURPRISES INTO OUR LIVES. ONE OF THOSE SURPRISES IS NEWS OF A BOY OR GIRL— OR ONE OF EACH! WHETHER YOU KNOW THE GENDER OF YOUR BABY OR NOT, TAKE A QUIET MOMENT TO CONSIDER YOUR THOUGHTS AND FEELINGS ABOUT IT. WHAT DID YOU NOTICE?

DESCRIBE WHAT YOU'D ENJOY ABOUT **HAVING A GIRL**.

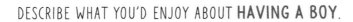

DESCRIBE WHAT YOU'D ENJOY ABOUT **HAVING A BOY**.

DESCRIBE WHAT YOU'D ENJOY ABOUT HAVING TWINS.

FOR WHAT ARE YOU GRATEFUL TODAY?

WHAT SMALL MIRACLES
MADE YOUR DAY BRIGHTER?

WRITE DOWN THREE THINGS YOU'VE ALREADY LEARNED ABOUT BEING A MOM.

1.

2.

3.

WRITE DOWN THREE THINGS YOU
HOPE TO LEARN ABOUT BEING A MOM.

1.

2.

3.

WHAT ARE YOU WISHING FOR TODAY?

Write your answers on the bright dandelions below.
Imagine blowing on the flowers one by one and
sending hopeful thoughts out into the world.

MAY YOUR CHOICES REFLECT YOUR HOPES, NOT YOUR FEARS.

—NELSON MANDELA

DESCRIBE, IN A FEW WORDS, THE PARENTING
TECHNIQUES, TRADITIONS, AND VALUES WITH WHICH
YOU WERE RAISED IN THE SPACE PROVIDED.

SPEND A FEW MINUTES CONSIDERING WHICH OF
THESE ELEMENTS YOU'D LIKE TO PASS ON.

CHART YOUR OWN COURSE AS A PARENT. At the center of the bullseye, write the values that you most want to instill. Fill in the remaining circles with more of your values and traditions until your parenting goals are fully represented.

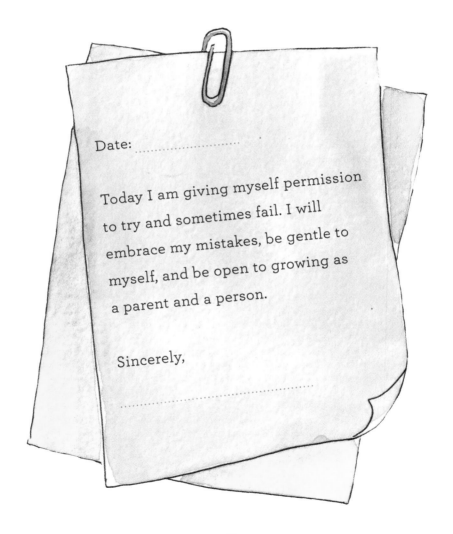

Date: ....

Today I am giving myself permission to try and sometimes fail. I will embrace my mistakes, be gentle to myself, and be open to growing as a parent and a person.

Sincerely,

....

The most important point is to ACCEPT YOURSELF AND STAND ON YOUR TWO FEET.

—SHUNRYU SUZUKI

WHAT DOES PREGNANCY FEEL LIKE TO YOU? TAKE A MOMENT TO WRITE YOUR ANSWER IN ONE OF THE THOUGHT BUBBLES BELOW. ASK YOUR PARTNER TO DO THE SAME.

WHILE YOUR PARTNER MAY NOT UNDERSTAND EXACTLY WHAT YOU'RE GOING THROUGH, speaking your truth can strengthen your bond and lighten your burden. Make time to express yourself to your partner or someone you love today.

How are your experiences similar or different?

How might your relationship benefit from these check-ins?

SOME OF THE BEST THINGS IN LIFE ARE BEAUTIFULLY FLAWED.

CHOOSE YOUR FAVORITES FROM THIS LIST
OF PERFECTLY IMPERFECT THINGS:

A CHILD SINGING OFF-KEY

THE WRINKLED HAND OF A LOVED ONE

THE ROUGH DRAFT OF A FAMOUS NOVEL

YOUR HOME AFTER A GATHERING OF FRIENDS

WHAT ITEMS FROM YOUR HOME OR LIFE COULD YOU ADD TO THIS LIST?

IMPERFECTION INSPIRES INVENTION,
IMAGINATION, CREATIVITY. . . .
THE MORE I FEEL IMPERFECT,
the more I feel alive.

—JHUMPA LAHIRI

USE YOUR NATURAL CREATIVITY TO DESIGN
OR PLAN THE SPACE WHERE YOUR BABY WILL
SLEEP AND PLAY. WHAT SYMBOLS OR COLORS WOULD YOU
LIKE TO INCLUDE? WHAT FAMILY PHOTOS, CHILDHOOD BOOKS,
OR KEEPSAKES SHOULD BE PART OF THIS SPACE?

WHAT MATTERS MOST TO YOU? HOW MIGHT THIS
INFORM THE LOOK AND FEEL OF THE BABY'S ROOM?

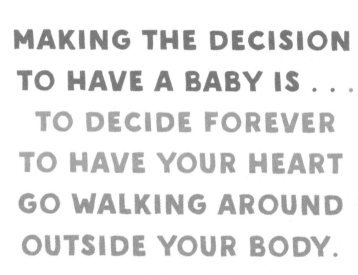

MAKING THE DECISION TO HAVE A BABY IS . . . TO DECIDE FOREVER TO HAVE YOUR HEART GO WALKING AROUND OUTSIDE YOUR BODY.

—ELIZABETH STONE

WHAT ARE SOME OF THE
STRONGEST BONDS IN YOUR LIFE?

WHEN HAVE YOU GIVEN YOUR
WHOLE HEART TO SOMEONE?

EVERY DAY HAS ITS SHARE OF ROSES, BUDS,
AND THORNS. STOP TO CONSIDER YOURS AS A WAY OF ADDING
MEANING AND REFLECTION TO A REGULAR DAY.

ROSE
(BEST MOMENT)

BUD
(FUTURE MOMENT I LOOK FORWARD TO)

THORN
(TOUGHEST MOMENT)

SEIZE THE OPPORTUNITY EVERY EVENING TO SMELL
THE ROSES, WATER THE BUDS, AND REMOVE THE THORNS

LIFE IS

A SUCCESSION OF LESSONS WHICH MUST BE LIVED TO BE UNDERSTOOD.

—RALPH WALDO EMERSON

WHAT DO YOU TURN TO when you need guidance,
advice, or reassurance? Circle any and all that apply.

BOOKS

FRIENDS

FAMILY

PARTNER

GUT INSTINCT

RELIGION

What lesson have you learned recently?

Find your happy

BEGINNING AND ENDING YOUR DAY
WITH THE SAME ACTION OR RITUAL IS A SIMPLE WAY
TO BRING SATISFACTION AND PEACE TO YOUR LIFE.

CHECK OFF ANY RITUALS BELOW THAT WOULD HELP YOU
EMBRACE THE DAY IN ALL ITS PERFECT IMPERFECTION:

A SHORT WALK

A FREE-WRITING SESSION TO CLEAR YOUR MIND

STATING ONE THING YOU'RE GRATEFUL FOR

REPEATING A HOPEFUL MANTRA

TALKING TO YOUR BABY

ADD YOUR OWN IDEAS HERE:

WHO OR WHAT
INSPIRES YOU?

MAKE MEANINGFUL CHOICES TODAY. INSTEAD OF APPROACHING THE DAY WITH A TO-DO LIST OF GOALS, MAKE TIME FOR LAUGHTER, INSPIRATION, AND HUMAN CONNECTION. WHAT OPPORTUNITIES FOR JOY WILL YOU ADD TO YOUR DAY?

RELEASE ANY ANXIETIES AND WORRIES YOU MAY BE HOLDING IN. Anxieties and worries are usually founded in fear. The more you learn to address these thoughts and follow them to their roots, the less power they will have over you. Write three things you're anxious about below:

1.

2.

3.

How might these anxieties say more about your insecurities than any real dangers ahead?

NOTHING EVER GOES AWAY

until it has taught us what we need to know.

—PEMA CHÖDRÖN

FIND A HEALTHY BALANCE between control and
surrender as you approach the birth of your child.
What do you find yourself trying to control?

How can you loosen the reins a little
and surrender to the experience?

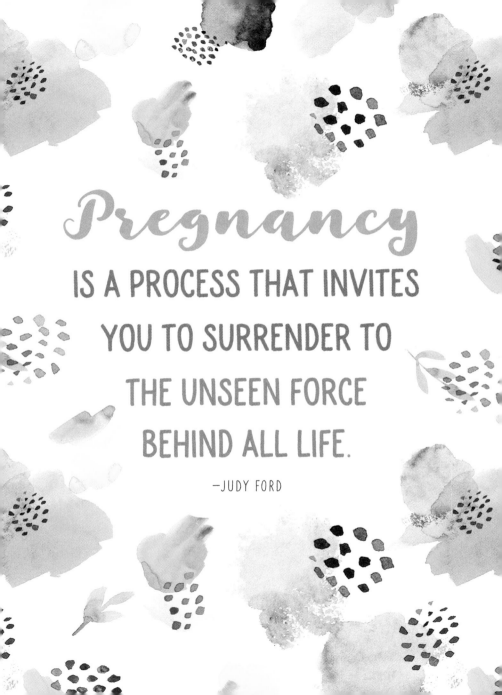

Pregnancy

IS A PROCESS THAT INVITES YOU TO SURRENDER TO THE UNSEEN FORCE BEHIND ALL LIFE.

—JUDY FORD

If you are at peace, you are living in the present.

—LAO TZU

As your pregnancy progresses, your thoughts will naturally gravitate toward the future and the day you get to meet your baby. This current moment, whether it's spirit-soaring, exhausting, enlightening, or just meh, will never come again. Color in the words below to remind yourself of the value of right now:

WHEREVER YOU ARE,
IT'S THE PLACE
YOU NEED TO BE.

—MAXIME LAGACÉ

In what ways does this ring true for you?

FIND YOUR GLOW

WHAT ARE THE ACTIVITIES, PEOPLE, OR CIRCUMSTANCES THAT MAKE YOU GLOW? ADD YOUR OWN TO THE LIST OF POSSIBILITIES BELOW.

LAUGHTER

FEELING THE BABY MOVE

A GOOD NIGHT'S SLEEP

EXERCISE

SPENDING TIME IN THE NURSERY

. . . .

WHEN, DURING YOUR PREGNANCY, HAVE YOU FELT MOST BEAUTIFUL? HOW CAN YOU FEEL THIS WAY MORE OFTEN?

WRITE ALL OF THE INSPIRING AND KIND WORDS that have guided you through pregnancy on the quilt below. Let this patchwork of compliments bring comfort and reassurance whenever you need it.

TREAT YOURSELF WITH KINDNESS. Pay attention to the way you talk to yourself today. What kinds of messages did you send to yourself? Did they match the tone of the words on the quilt?

Throughout the day strive to be as kind
to yourself as you are to your own best friends.
Write a few kind words to yourself below.

PRACTICE A SITTING MEDITATION WITH YOUR BABY TODAY.

Find a chair that allows you to sit with your back straight and your feet flat on the floor. Pay attention to your breath. As you breathe in through your nose, imagine that you are taking all the love and hope in the world into your body and sharing it with your baby.

When you breathe out through your mouth, imagine that you are expelling any stress in your body. Do this for as long as you like until you feel refreshed and at peace.

WRITE ALL THE WAYS IN WHICH YOU'D LIKE TO BOND WITH YOUR BABY WHEN HE/SHE ARRIVES.

WHAT ALONE TIME OR FAVORITE ACTIVITIES WILL YOU RESERVE FOR YOURSELF WHEN THE BABY IS BORN?

ACKNOWLEDGING HOW YOU FEEL
IS ONE WAY TO PRACTICE MINDFULNESS.

Color in the empty bottle below to reflect how positive your
thoughts are in this moment.

How can you add more love and laughter to your day?

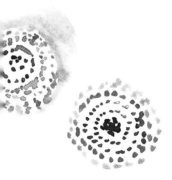

BE AUTHENTICALLY YOU TODAY AND EVERY DAY.

Focus on your best qualities and celebrate the quirks that make you real (and all the more lovable). Finish the phrases below with encouraging and honest words about the amazing person you are.

I'M INCREDIBLE BECAUSE

· ·

I'M BEAUTIFUL WHEN I

· ·

I'M A NATURAL AT

· ·

I'M GOING TO BE A

· **MOM.**

WHO YOU ARE IS ALWAYS RIGHT.

—DENG MING—DAO

IMAGINE THAT YOU ARE THE SKY ON THIS PAGE.
WHETHER IT'S A BEAMING SUN, A DRIZZLING RAIN,
OR A QUIET SNOWFALL, DRAW YOUR CURRENT MOOD ALL OVER
THIS PAGE. CONSIDER THE TEMPORARY WEATHER OF YOUR
FEELINGS AND THE PERMANENCE OF THE SKY.

CLOSE YOUR EYES AND DO A FULL-BODY MINDFULNESS SCAN
FROM THE TOP OF YOUR HEAD TO THE SOLES OF YOUR FEET.
CHECK IN WITH A DIFFERENT PART OF YOUR BODY WITH EVERY BREATH IN
AND RELAX, OR SOFTEN IT, AS YOU BREATHE OUT.

WHERE DO YOU FEEL
MOST RELAXED?
CIRCLE IT ON
THE IMAGE BELOW.

WHERE DO YOU
FEEL TIGHT OR
STRESSED? MARK
IT ON THE IMAGE
BELOW WITH AN X.

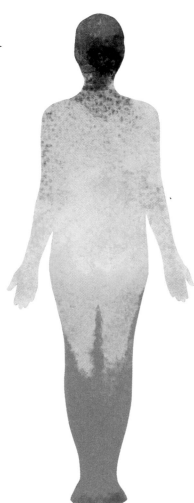

WHAT ARE YOUR BODY'S SIGNALS THAT YOU NEED TO REST?
HOW WELL DO YOU LISTEN TO THESE SIGNALS?

HOW CAN YOU ADD MORE BREAKS
OR RESTFUL MOMENTS TO YOUR DAY?

*A woman
is the
full circle.*
WITHIN HER IS
THE POWER TO CREATE,
NURTURE, AND TRANSFORM.

—DIANE MARIECHILD

Think of all the ways in which you have nurtured your baby and yourself during each trimester of your pregnancy and write them in the three sections of the circle below.

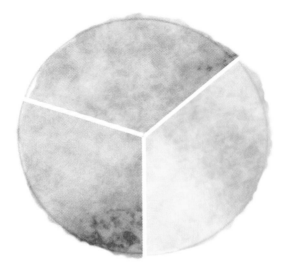

How has pregnancy transformed you (and your life) so far?

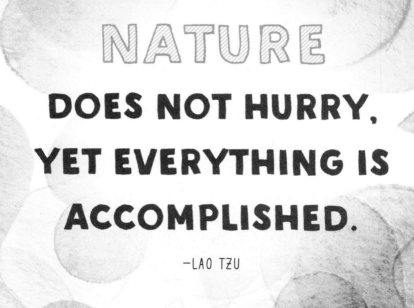

NATURE
DOES NOT HURRY,
YET EVERYTHING IS
ACCOMPLISHED.

—LAO TZU

MAKE A LIST OF WONDERFUL THINGS
IN NATURE THAT TAKE THEIR TIME:

RETURN TO THESE THOUGHTS WHEN YOU NEED
A REMINDER TO SLOW DOWN AND LET LIFE HAPPEN.

COLOR IN EACH OF THE SOCKS BELOW WITH A UNIQUE
COLOR OR PATTERN. NONE OF THEM WILL MATCH IN THE END,
BUT THAT'S OKAY. EMBRACE THE WILD ADVENTURE
OF PARENTHOOD AND LIVE LIFE AS YOU WANT TO LIVE IT.

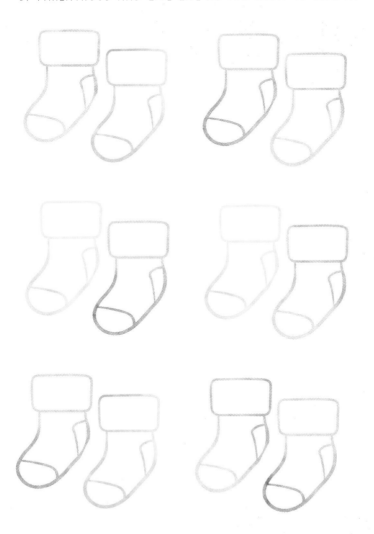

CHOOSE A SIMPLE ACTIVITY TO DO MINDFULLY TODAY.

It can be drinking tea, combing your hair, or washing dishes. Imagine, as you go through the motions, that this activity is the only thing in the entire universe that matters. Pay attention, for example, to the feeling of the warm teacup in the crook of your hand, the steam filling your nostrils, and the first note of the flavor on your tongue. Describe your mindful moment below:

Which parts of your pregnancy do you think you'll look back on most fondly?

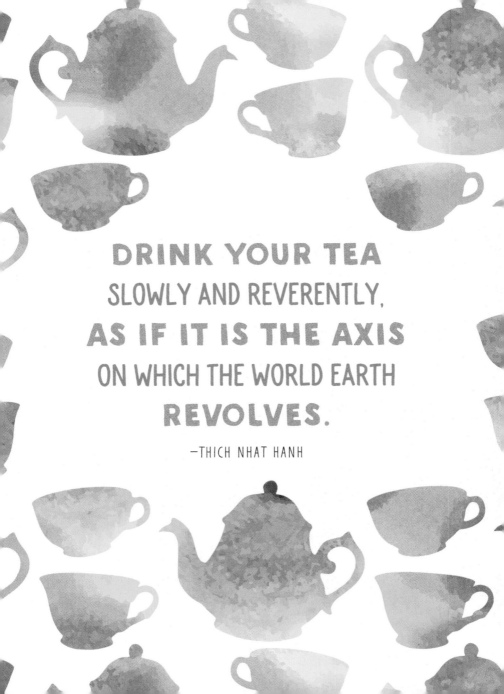

DRINK YOUR TEA
SLOWLY AND REVERENTLY,
AS IF IT IS THE AXIS
ON WHICH THE WORLD EARTH
REVOLVES.

—THICH NHAT HANH

It is only in still water

THAT WE SEE CLEARLY.

—TAOIST PROVERB

WHAT HAS PREGNANCY ALLOWED YOU TO SEE MORE CLEARLY?

WHAT DO YOU THINK YOU MIGHT ALREADY
KNOW ABOUT YOUR BABY?

DESCRIBE THE EXPERIENCE OF FEELING YOUR BABY MOVE.
WHAT WOULD YOU COMPARE IT TO?

WRITE THE WORDS OF YOUR
FAVORITE LULLABY OR SONG BELOW.

SING THESE WORDS TO YOUR BABY TODAY AND EVERY DAY
UNTIL YOU MEET ONE ANOTHER AT LAST.

WHEN YOU IMAGINE YOUR CHILD,
HOW DO YOU PICTURE HIM/HER?

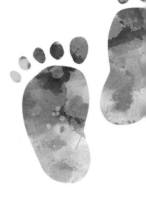

WHAT NAME OR NICKNAME HAVE YOU
ALREADY GIVEN YOUR BABY?

WHEN DOES THE REALITY OF MEETING
YOUR LITTLE ONE HIT HOME?

WRITE A HOPE YOU HAVE FOR YOUR BABY'S FUTURE ON EACH OF THE STARS BELOW.

WHAT DO YOU KNOW YOU CAN GIVE TO YOUR BABY?

WHAT WILL YOU TEACH YOUR BABY ABOUT
LIFE, LOVE, AND HAPPINESS?

My Baby

NAME:

DATE
OF BIRTH:

LENGTH:

WEIGHT:

HOW IT FELT TO HOLD MY BABY FOR THE FIRST TIME:

HOW I FEEL NOW, IN THIS MOMENT: